THE
SLAVE TRADE
AND THE MIDDLE PASSAGE

DRAMA OF AFRICAN-AMERICAN HISTORY

The SLAVE TRADE AND THE MIDDLE PASSAGE

by S. PEARL SHARP
with VIRGINIA SCHOMP

Marshall Cavendish
Benchmark
New York

ACKNOWLEDGMENTS

I follow, with great awe and trepidation, in the domain of several black historians who dedicated their lives to revealing the truth to their people, no matter what the personal or professional cost. This work is a thank-you note to Ivan Van Sertima, Dr. Ben (Yosef ben-Jochannan), Runoko Rashidi, and the ancestors John Henrik Clarke, Chancellor Williams, Edward Scobie, and Arthur Schomburg. And I am humbly grateful to every librarian on the planet.

With gratitude, also, to Jill Watts, professor of history at California State University, San Marcos, for her perceptive comments on the manuscript, and to the late Richard Newman, civil rights advocate, author, and senior research officer at the W.E.B. DuBois Institute at Harvard University, for his excellent work in formulating the series.

EDITOR: JOYCE STANTON   EDITORIAL DIRECTOR: MICHELLE BISSON
ART DIRECTOR: ANAHID HAMPARIAN   SERIES DESIGNER: MICHAEL NELSON

MARSHALL CAVENDISH BENCHMARK 99 WHITE PLAINS ROAD TARRYTOWN, NEW YORK 10591-9001 www.marshallcavendish.us Text copyright © 2007 by S. Pearl Sharp Map copyright © 2007 by Mike Reagan All rights reserved. No part of this book may be reproduced or utilized in any form or by any means electronic or mechanical including photocopying, recording, or by any information storage and retrieval system, without permission from the copyright holders. All Internet sites were available and accurate when this book was sent to press. LIBRARY OF CONGRESS CATALOGING-IN-PUBLICATION DATA: Sharp, S. Pearl. The slave trade and the middle passage / by S. Pearl Sharp with Virginia Schomp. p. cm. — (Drama of African-American history) Summary: "Traces the history of the transatlantic slave trade and the development of slavery in the New World"—Provided by publisher. Includes bibliographical references and index. ISBN-13: 978-0-7614-2176-4 ISBN-10: 0-7614-2176-9 1. Slave trade—America—History—Juvenile literature. 2. Slavery—America—History—Juvenile literature. 3. Slave trade—Africa—History—Juvenile literature. I. Schomp, Virginia. II. Title. III. Series. HT1049.S43 2007 306.3'62097—dc22 200600532

Images provided by Rose Corbett Gordon, Art Editor, Mystic CT, from the following sources: Cover: North Wind Picture Archives Back cover: Michael Graham-Stewart/ Bridgeman Art Library Page i: State of Connecticut; pages ii - iii, 46: The Art Archive/Private Collection/Marc Charmet; pages vi, 30, 59: Hulton Archive/Getty Images; pages vii, 16: The Art Archive/Bibliothèque des Arts Decoratifs Paris/Dagli Orti; page viii: Amistad America; page x: Stapleton Collection/Corbis; page 2: Massachusetts Historical Society, Boston/ Bridgeman Art Library; page 4: Roger-Viollet/Topham/The Image Works; page 6: Historical Picture Archive/Corbis; pages 8, 52: Michael Graham-Stewart/ Bridgeman Art Library; page 10 top: The Art Archive/Museo de Arte Antiga Lisbon/Dagli Orti; page 10 bottom: Werner Forman/Art Resource, NY; page 11: The Art Archive/Marine Museum Lisbon/Dagli Orti; page 14: The Art Archive/Dagli Orti; page 17: Beinecke Rare Book and Manuscript Library, Yale University; page 18: Cover to the work The Negro's Memorial, or Abolitionist's Catechism located in the Rare Book, Manuscript, and Special Collections Library, Duke University, with scan provided by Documenting the American South (http://docsouth.unc.edu), The University of North Carolina at Chapel Hill Libraries; page 20: The Stapleton Collection/ Bridgeman Art Library; page 22: Victoria & Albert Museum/Art Resource, NY; pages 23, 55: Bettmann/Corbis; page 25: Francis G. Mayer/Corbis; page 27: The Art Archive/Museo Diocesano Orta/Dagli Orti; pages 28, 32, 44: Mary Evans Picture Library/The Image Works; page 29: American Jewish Historical Society, Newton Centre, Massachusetts and New York, New York; page 37 top: Brooks Kraft/Corbis; page 37 bottom: AFP/Getty Images; page 39: The Art Archive/Maritime Museum Kronberg Castle Denmark/Dagli Orti; pages 42, 51: Mel Fisher Maritime Heritage Society, Inc.; page 48: The Art Archive/Musé du Nouveau Monde La Rochelle; page 54: The Art Archive/Culver Pictures/Dagli Orti; page 55: Bettmann/Corbis; page 56: Wilberforce House, Hull City Museums and Art Galleries, UK/ Bridgeman Art Library; page 57: The Art Archive/Eileen Tweedy; page 60: Giraudon/Art Resource, NY; page 63: Nik Wheeler/Corbis; page 65: Time Life Pictures/Getty Images

Printed in China

3 5 6 4 2

Front cover: African captives on board a slave ship
Back cover: British sailors stop an illegal slave ship.
Title page: Slaves being forced to dance for their captors
p. vi: Africans captured by slave smugglers try to sleep in the cramped hold of a ship.

CONTENTS

INTRODUCTION

The Slave Trade and the Middle Passage is the second book in a series called the Drama of African-American History. The first book in this series was about Africa, the continent where the story of African Americans began. Now we will follow the people who were taken from Africa as slaves, tracing their journey across the Atlantic Ocean to the Americas.

The forced voyage of Africans across the Atlantic is usually called the transatlantic slave trade or Middle Passage. It also has been given other names that more adequately reflect the pain and hardship enslaved Africans endured. These terms include the Black Holocaust, the African Holocaust, and, in some African countries, *le mort,* from the French term for "death." Some African Americans may describe the experience of their ancestors with a word borrowed from the African language Swahili: *maafa,* meaning "disaster" or "great suffering."

The transatlantic slave trade was only one part of a long history of slavery in Africa. The practice existed on the continent even before the eighth century, when Arab traders began transporting African captives across the Sahara Desert to slave markets in North Africa, the Middle East, and India. Later, European slave traders carried Africans to Europe and its island colonies in the Atlantic Ocean. Finally, European and American traders brought enslaved Africans across the Atlantic to the Americas.

Europeans were first attracted to Africa for its gold and other rich natural resources. Beginning in the early 1400s, explorers, adventurers, and merchants sailed from Europe to West Africa to acquire gold, ivory, pepper, grain, animal hides, and other goods. At first trade ships carried their cargoes back to their home ports. Then Christopher Columbus and other European explorers found their way across the Atlantic Ocean to the Americas. The "discovery" of this New World led to new trading patterns. Ships began to follow a triangular trading route, sailing from Europe to Africa, then from Africa to European colonies in the

"Panning" for gold in 1820s Africa

Americas, and finally from the Americas back to Europe. The journey along the second side of this triangle was known as the Middle Passage. Sailing the Middle Passage was extremely difficult and dangerous. It would hardly have been worth the risks, except for the huge profits offered by the slave trade.

The New World required a seemingly endless supply of laborers to clear the land and work the fields. To satisfy that demand, traders imported millions of African slaves over a long period that lasted from the mid-1400s through the late 1800s. Over the course of those four centuries, slave ships made at least 54,000 voyages to Africa, mainly from Portugal, Spain, Britain, France, the Netherlands, and, later, the

A re-creation of the slave ship *Amistad*

United States. Approximately 30 million to 60 million Africans were captured, and about one-third of them survived to face enslavement. Because of the way the slave trade was conducted, those numbers are only estimates. There are few complete commercial records from the early years of the slave trade and hardly any from its final years, when the trade in human beings had been officially abolished but still continued illegally. Although the precise count will never be known, the toll in human life was obviously enormous.

The slave trade not only uprooted an immense number of people but also inflicted tremendous agony on its victims. Black men, women, and children were torn from their homelands, branded, chained, and forced onto ships where the living conditions were almost unimaginably harsh. Children and parents, husbands and wives, brothers and sisters were separated forever. Once on board a slave ship, only a few captives would ever see Africa again. Many would not even live to see the Americas. In fact, so many captured Africans died crossing the Atlantic in the crowded, filthy slave ships that it is sometimes said that a "railroad of bones" stretches across the ocean floor.

Today the story of the transatlantic slave trade may seem like ancient history, but the legacy of that terrible period is all around us. The slave trade brought about one of the most massive human migrations of all time, transforming the societies of Africa, Europe, and the Americas. In Africa physical remnants of the trade still remain. If you sailed a boat along the coast of West Africa, for example, you would see dozens of castle-like forts built by Europeans as centers for the buying and selling of human beings. In Europe and the Americas, the effects of the slave trade can be seen in the numerous contributions enslaved Africans made in areas including farming technology, cooking, healing techniques, textiles, art, music, dance, and literature.

In addition, many issues concerning the slave trade remain relevant today. Scholars and historians continue to debate questions about the Africans' involvement in their own enslavement and whether the slave trade developed mainly out of racism or economic forces. Americans continue to confront the contradictions of having built a "free society" on the backs of slaves. Finally, the lingering effects of slavery and the slave trade live on in the experiences, emotions, and beliefs of many descendants of both the enslavers and the enslaved.

SPECIAL TERMS

As you read this book, remember that language is flexible and changes over time. In quotations from works written in earlier centuries, you may come across some odd-looking spellings, punctuation, capitalization, and grammar. Also keep in mind this book's special usage of a few terms:

Africans as used here refers to Africans of color, including people from tribal groups such as the Mende, Songhai, Bantu, Ashanti, Fon, and Ibo.

Negro, which comes from the Spanish word for "black," was a term once used throughout the Western world to refer to a black person, so it sometimes appears in quoted passages.

Americas means the geographic region that includes North America, Central America, South America, Greenland, and the Caribbean islands (also known as the West Indies). This region may also be called the New World or the Western Hemisphere.

Chapter 1

The New World and the New Slavery

BEFORE EUROPEANS FOUND THEIR WAY TO SUB-Saharan Africa in the early 1400s, slavery and the slave trade existed there. Since ancient times the people of many African societies had enslaved fellow Africans captured in war. In addition, for at least eight hundred years, Arab merchants had been crossing northern Africa on camels to conduct the trans-Saharan slave trade. Traveling west from the Red Sea all the way across the Sahara, these merchants traded with African slaveholders, exchanging spices, textiles, horses, and other goods for slaves. The African slaves acquired by Arab traders were taken primarily to markets in the Arabian Peninsula and other lands in Asia.

Under the system of slavery practiced in Africa, captives were usually entitled to some rights and liberties. Their masters

1

Slaves in a West African village celebrate a wedding; in Africa, slaves had rights and privileges that they did not enjoy in Europe and the Americas.

had to provide them with food, clothing, shelter, and protection. African slaves could marry and own property. Their obligation to their owners usually had an ending date, which made this form of slavery similar to indentured servitude, a system in which a person agrees to work for a master for a specific number of years. Most importantly, the slave's status was not hereditary. That meant that the children of slaves were born free.

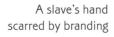

A slave's hand scarred by branding

The first African slaves taken to the New World were also treated much like indentured servants. Like white indentured workers, these Africans had some basic rights and protections, and they were usually set free after their term of service ended. (Often, though, their terms of service were longer than those of whites.) Gradually a new and much harsher system known as chattel slavery developed for blacks. Under this system a slave was actually owned by the slaveholder, just like a farm animal or a piece of furniture. The indenture of chattel slaves was extended to a lifetime. Eventually slavery became a status inherited by their children.

As the social standing of black slaves decreased, the cruelty inflicted on them increased. Their living quarters were often little better than the sheds or stalls where the farm animals were kept. Like animals, they might be branded, whipped, and chained. It was legal for a master to mutilate or kill a slave.

SLAVERY AND RACE

Did the transatlantic slave trade grow out of economics or racism? In debating that question, historians consider several facts.

The first Africans in the American colonies were often treated the same way as European indentured servants. They performed the same jobs, received equal punishments, and usually had the same opportunities to earn or buy their freedom, although frequently their terms of indenture were longer than those of whites. Soon, however, the situation began to change: while indenture continued to apply to white laborers, it turned into lifelong servitude for blacks.

Further, in the 1600s there was a gradual change in the way European colonists defined themselves and others. Early colonists thought of a person as Christian or non-Christian; master or servant; Englishman, Dutchman, or African. Over time another distinction became even more important: white or black. In 1640 three indentured servants were captured after running away from their master's farm in Virginia. A court sentenced the two white servants to four additional years of service as punishment. The black servant was condemned to a lifetime of slavery.

The evidence seems to show that European colonists in the Americas chose slavery because of its economic benefits. However, the sole factor determining who could be permanently enslaved was the color of his or her skin.

Francis Le Jau, a missionary sent from England to colonial North America in 1706, was shocked by the brutal treatment of captive Africans. "A poor slavewoman was barbarously burnt alive near my door without any positive proof of the Crime she was accused of," wrote Le Jau. "Many Masters can't be persuaded that Negroes . . . are otherwise than beasts, and use them like such." David George, who was born into slavery in Virginia in the early 1740s, recalled the cruel beatings that all the members of his family received from their master. His oldest sister, Patty, was whipped so often that

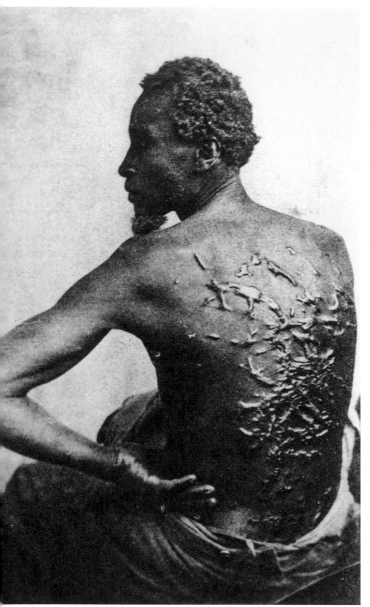

This man's scars from numerous whippings bear witness to the cruelty of the slave system. The photo was taken in Louisiana in 1863.

> her back [was] all corruption, as though it would rot. . . . I also have been whipped many a time on my naked skin, and sometimes till the blood has run down over my waistband: but the greatest grief I then had was to see them whip my mother, and to hear her, on her knees, begging for mercy.

THE PROMISE OF THE NEW WORLD

To Europeans, the New World "discovered" by Christopher Columbus seemed like the answer to many Old World problems. During the sixteenth century, Europe experienced significant changes and challenges. The population was growing, so that at some times and places there were more people than the land could support. Power struggles caused upheavals in government. Religious freedom was often restricted or denied.

Because of these factors, hosts of Europeans were willing to face hardship and uncertainty in hopes of a brighter future in the New World. Many settlers came to the Americas as indentured servants, signing contracts that required them to work for a master for an average of four to seven years, in return for transportation, food, clothing, and shelter. Other settlers were forced to emigrate. For example, criminals might be offered a "choice" between hanging or a period of labor in the colonies. In some cases people were falsely accused of crimes to force them into indenture.

The colonists who settled in the New World remained under the government and authority of their home countries. They might be sent to claim a new territory for their homeland or to develop an area that had been previously claimed. Often these areas were already inhabited. The Europeans called the native inhabitants of North America "Indians." As the Europeans founded colonies, they seized control of the Indians' homelands and then exploited the land and the people for their own benefit.

British colonists who settled in the northern regions of North America usually divided the confiscated lands into small farms. Farther south, in places such as Virginia and South Carolina, Brazil, and the islands of the Caribbean, most of the fertile lands were converted into plantations. These vast farm

Slaves at work on a tobacco plantation, preparing the crop for market

estates usually specialized in a single crop, such as sugarcane, coffee, or tobacco.

Clearing fields, raising crops, building shelters, and all the other tasks of developing the land were hard and exhausting work. On the southern plantations especially, there were never enough white laborers to meet the planters' needs. At first, many plantation owners filled out their labor force with Native Americans. The Indian laborers, however, grew sick and died from diseases such as measles and smallpox, which were brought to the Americas by Europeans. In Europe people were usually exposed to these diseases as children, and the bodies of survivors developed a natural resistance. The Indians had no such immunity.

To replace the Indian labor force, colonists began to import enslaved Africans. The goods produced by these laborers benefited the economy of European nations. With their increased wealth, Europeans could afford to buy more of the new and varied products available in the New World. That created a need for larger plantations, which in return increased the demand for laborers. This spiraling cycle of supply and demand would spur on the transatlantic slave trade, changing life in Europe, the Americas, and Africa forever.

A young boy enslaved
and chained in an
African city in the
late 1800s

Chapter 2

PLANTING THE SEEDS

In 1767 young Ottobah Cugoano of Ghana, West Africa, went to visit an uncle who lived three days' walk from his home. Ottobah spent many happy days among the children of his uncle's village. The boys and girls often ventured into the woods, where they chased the birds and gathered wild fruit. One day, as Ottobah and his friends were playing, several raiders appeared. The children tried to run away, but the men threatened them with knives and pistols. Dividing the captives into small groups, the raiders led them far from their homes.

PORTUGAL ESTABLISHES THE SLAVE TRADE

The kidnapping and enslaving of Ottobah Cugoano and his companions by slave raiders was part of a brutal practice that had been taking place for more than three hundred years.

Prince Henry the Navigator sponsored many Portuguese voyages to West Africa.

The Portuguese built Elmina Castle in 1482 as a base for the slave trade.

Portugal was the first European trader in African slaves. In the mid-1400s the Portuguese fleet ruled the seas. Prince Henry of Portugal, also known as Henry the Navigator, sent his nation's swift, sturdy sailing vessels on many voyages of exploration and discovery. Portuguese explorers traveled all along the west coast of Africa, often stopping to trade for gold, animal skins, and other goods. In 1441 one ambitious captain captured twelve Africans and carried them back to Henry. The following year Portuguese seamen brought home another small group of captives. And so it went, year after year, with Europeans swooping down and carrying off African men, women, and children.

By the end of the fifteenth century, Portuguese and Spanish slave traders had abducted nearly 200,000 Africans and sold them into bondage. The first of many slaving centers, a fortress known as Elmina Castle, had been built in Ghana along the West African coast. The seeds had been planted for the transatlantic slave trade.

EUROPEANS FIGHT FOR DOMINANCE

In 1492 Columbus's voyage to the New World established Spain as a rival sea power. To prevent war between Spain and Portugal, Pope Alexander VI commanded the two powers to divide the world, except for the Christian nations of Europe, between them. The result was the Treaty of Tordesillas, signed in 1494. The treaty divided the globe along an imaginary line running north and south through the Atlantic Ocean and South America. Portugal's half included Africa as well as much

of Brazil. The rest of the New World would belong to Spain.

The Treaty of Tordesillas ensured Portugal's control of the African slave trade for the next two centuries. At first, Spain relied on Portuguese slave traders to supply captive Africans to the Spanish colonies in the New World. Then Spain's rulers began a system of contracts known as *asiento,* from the Spanish word for "agreement." These special licenses were granted to selected traders, companies, or nations, giving them the exclusive right to supply Spain's American colonies with slaves.

As the other nations of Europe saw the rich profits flowing from the slave trade, they began to challenge Spanish-Portuguese dominance. France entered the competition in the mid-1500s and eventually established a stronghold on the coast of Senegal in western Africa. Britain exported vast numbers of Africans from slave trading posts near the mouth of the Gambia River in the same region and from southern Africa. The

Diplomats from Spain and Portugal negotiate to divide the New World and Africa between their two nations, under the oversight of the pope (seated on the left).

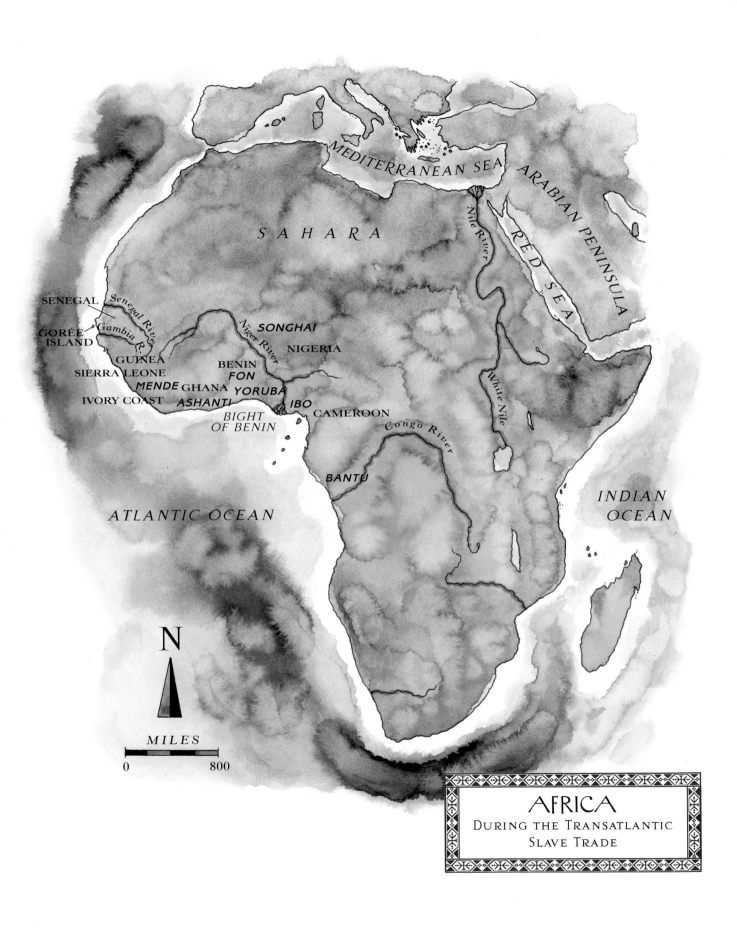

MEDITERRANEAN SEA

ARABIAN PENINSULA

SAHARA

Nile River

RED SEA

SENEGAL

Senegal River

GORÉE
ISLAND

Gambia R.

SONGHAI

Niger River

NIGERIA

GUINEA

BENIN

SIERRA LEONE

FON

MENDE

GHANA

YORUBA

White Nile

IVORY COAST

ASHANTI

IBO

CAMEROON

BIGHT
OF BENIN

Congo River

BANTU

INDIAN
OCEAN

ATLANTIC OCEAN

N

MILES

0   800

AFRICA
DURING THE TRANSATLANTIC
SLAVE TRADE

Netherlands seized control of numerous slave centers on the West African coast following wars with Portugal in the mid-1600s. In time Belgium, Germany, Denmark, and nearly every other European power would play a role in the transatlantic slave trade.

Capture and Delivery

In the early days of the slave trade, most Africans were seized in raids along the west coast. As the demand for slaves increased, more and more captives were taken from the interior of west and west-central Africa.

Captives seized by slave raiders in the African interior faced a long journey to the coast. In 1738 English slave trader Francis Moore observed that the raiders' "way of bringing [captives] is, tying them by the neck with leather thongs, at about a yard distance from each other, 30 or 40 in a string." The long lines of bound captives might walk for weeks or even months from one holding site to the next, urged on by the whips of their captors. Thousands died during these forced marches. Some captives perished from hunger, thirst, illness, injury, or exhaustion. Others were beaten to death. Those who survived the journey were sometimes so sick and weak when they arrived at the coast that no trader would buy them. Rejected captives were often treated "with great severity," wrote British ship's surgeon Alexander Falconbridge. "It matters not whether they are refused on account of age, illness, deformity or for any other reason. . . . The traders have frequently been known to put them to death. Instances have happened . . . , when negroes have been objected to, that the traders have . . . instantly beheaded them."

Rooms where captives were held while awaiting slave ships on Gorée Island, off the coast of Senegal

Slaves who were judged "good and sound" were branded with knives or red-hot irons. According to British slave trader John Barbot, this practice made it easy for the buyers to "distinguish their own, and to prevent [the slaves'] being chang'd by the natives for worse, as they are apt [likely] to do. . . . Care is taken that the women, as tenderest, be not burnt too hard." Then the captives were placed in primitive holding pens called "slave factories" or "warehouses" until a ship arrived to transport them across the Atlantic.

After Ottobah Cugoano was kidnapped, he and his companions were led to a town where they saw their first white people. Ottobah was terrified, because the children of his inland village had always been told that whites were cannibals. Following a restless night, the boy awoke to the sound of cries. He saw a number of African men, chained in a line, with their hands cuffed or tied behind their backs. Ottobah and the other captives walked a long way to a castle by the sea. There the captive Africans were forced to board a ship. Those who resisted were whipped and beaten. "It was a most horrible scene," Ottobah later recalled. "There was nothing to be heard but rattling of chains, smacking of whips, and the groans and cries of our fellow-men."

THE HUMAN MAP

The capture of Africans and their forced migration throughout the Americas created what one historian has called a "map of human geography." Africans enslaved through the transatlantic slave trade were sent mainly to three parts of the New World. About 58 percent went to Central and South America, with two-thirds of these going to Brazil. About 37 percent were sent to the West Indies, and about 5 percent went to mainland North America, including the colonies that would eventually become the United States.

Some of the Africans transported to the New World worked in gold and silver mines. Some planted and harvested rice, hauled loads of tobacco, picked coffee beans and cocoa beans, or cultivated indigo plants, which were used to make a deep blue dye for textiles. The main force driving the transatlantic slave trade, however, was sugar.

Before the 1500s sugar was very scarce and expensive in Europe. Then colonists found that they could cultivate sugarcane in the fertile tropics of the Americas. The highly prized crop quickly became one of the world's most important and profitable trade items.

The dominant sugar-producing centers were Brazil, Cuba,

A slave cutting sugarcane on a plantation in the West Indies in 1799

and the West Indies islands of Barbados, Jamaica, and Hispaniola (today's Haiti and the Dominican Republic). As the demand for sugar skyrocketed, plantation owners in those areas often converted their fields from other crops to sugarcane. Jamaica was covered by vast sugarcane plantations, making the island the world's largest sugar producer. Barbados, left with no room for any crops except sugar, was forced to import most of its food from England.

Millions of enslaved Africans labored on the huge sugar plantations, which often sprawled over two hundred acres or more. Planting, harvesting, and processing sugarcane was hot, dangerous, backbreaking work. Plantation owners worked their slaves from dawn to dusk and even longer at harvesttime. They did little to ensure their workers' health or safety. It was easier and cheaper to work slaves to death and then replace them. According to British slave ship captain John Newton, the owners of sugar plantations on the island of Antigua carefully compared the different methods of managing slaves. Was it more economical "to appoint them moderate work, plenty of provision, and such treatment as might enable them to protract their lives to old age? Or, by rigorously straining their strength to the utmost, with little relaxation, hard fare, and hard usage, to wear them out before they became useless and unable to do service, and then, to buy new ones, to fill up their places?" According to "these skilful calculations," said Newton, the second method

FINDING THE WAY HOME

Of the millions of enslaved Africans who came to the New World, hardly any would see home again. Margru, a young girl from Sierra Leone, was one of the few captives who did manage to return to Africa. Margru was sold to Spanish slave traders in the 1830s by her family in order to repay a debt. She was about seven years old. Along with five hundred other captives, she endured a two-month journey by slave ship to Havana, Cuba. In 1839 Margru was traveling down the Cuban coast on another ship, the *Amistad,* when one of the most famous slave mutinies in history took place. (For more about the *Amistad,* see chapter 5.)

While the leaders of the *Amistad* mutiny awaited trial, Margru lived with a family in Connecticut. She learned English, converted to Christianity, and took the name Sarah Kinson. Eventually the girl was set free and returned to Sierra Leone with a group of missionaries. At age fifteen she came back to the United States to attend Oberlin College in Ohio. Although she was an excellent student, she was terribly homesick. "Africa is my home," she confided in a letter to a friend. "I long to be there. Although I am in America, yet my heart is there [with] the people I love and the country I admire." After completing her education in 1849, Sarah Margru Kinson returned home once again to work as a missionary and teacher.

Above: A sketch of Margru, made when she was young

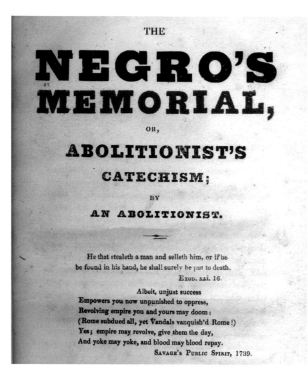

Ottobah Cugoano's story of his enslavement appeared in this abolitionist publication in 1787. Narratives such as Cugoano's played an important role in convincing Europeans and Americans of the evils of slavery.

was found to be "much the cheaper." As a result, on many plantations, "it was seldom known that a slave had lived above nine years."

The enslavement and forced migration of millions of Africans changed the human landscape in Africa and the Americas. By the mid-1800s, Africans and their descendants made up roughly 50 percent of the population of Cuba. In Barbados the ratio of blacks to whites was about three to one. In Jamaica it was ten to one. Slaveholders worried about these growing black populations. Hoping to prevent slave uprisings, they punished rebellious slaves with increasing cruelty and placed ever-greater restrictions on both slaves and free blacks. Plantation owner William Byrd of Virginia, who frequently whipped his slaves to keep them in line, wrote about the "pub-lick danger" posed by the growing number of slaves:

> Their Numbers increase every day as well by birth as importation. And in case there should arise a Man of desperate courage amongst us, exasper-ated by a desperate fortune [fate], he might . . . kindle a Servile [slave] War. Such a man might be dreadfully mischievous before any opposition could be formed against him, and tinge our Rivers as wide as they are with blood.

Ottobah Cugoano was taken by slave slip to a plantation in Granada, southern Spain, where he labored in "dreadful captivity and horrible slavery, without any hope of deliverance." But Cugoano was more fortunate than most enslaved Africans. After nine months a man who was returning to England took the boy with him as his personal servant. In England Cugoano began to teach himself to read and write. His master sent him to school and eventually granted his freedom. In 1787 Ottobah Cugoano published Thoughts and Sentiments on the Evil and Wicked Traffic of the Commerce of the Human Species, *the first major antislavery text written in English by an African.*

Sir John Hawkins was a naval hero and brave sailor, but he was also England's first slave trader.

Chapter 3

SLAVERY TAKES ROOT

FIRST ONE NATION AND THEN ANOTHER PULLED AHEAD in the international competition for control of Africa and the Americas. Through contracts, patents, decrees, and laws, the slave trade came to be strictly regulated. What had started out as a small, haphazard operation quickly grew into a well-organized, ever-expanding institution.

BRITAIN GAINS THE UPPER HAND

Nearly every European power played a role in shipping African slaves to the New World. However, the winner by far of the international competition for control of the slave trade was Great Britain.

British involvement in the African slave trade began with an ambitious sea captain named John Hawkins. In 1562 Hawkins sailed to West Africa in defiance of the Spanish *asiento*. The captain seized three hundred captives and carried them to the Spanish West Indies, where he traded them for sugar and other products to sell in England. Over the next ten years, Hawkins organized at least three other slaving journeys. His ventures earned substantial profits not only for the British merchants who financed them but also for members of the court of Queen Elizabeth I. The queen eventually granted Hawkins a knighthood in reward for his services to England. His coat of arms featured a bound African slave.

Queen Elizabeth also issued the first patent authorizing the founding of a British colony in the New World. That royal grant went to Sir Walter Raleigh. In 1585 Raleigh sponsored the voyage of British colonists to Roanoke Island, in present-day North Carolina. After a year of drought, hunger, and battles with neighboring Indians, the wilderness colony was abandoned. A second group of colonists, sent to revive the Roanoke settlement in 1587, vanished without a trace. In 1607 the British attempted to found another colony in the North American wilderness, at the mouth of the Kennebec River in Maine. Within a year, the harsh weather and Indian attacks had driven the Kennebec settlers back to England.

The English slave trade began during the reign of Queen Elizabeth I.

Britain's first permanent settlement in North America was Jamestown, Virginia, established in 1607. The early Jamestown colonists also endured terrible hardships. However, ships bearing supplies and new settlers helped the struggling colony sur-

AMERICA'S FIRST AFRICANS

In 1619 twenty black captives arrived in the Jamestown colony. They were the first permanent African settlers in an English colony, but they were not the first Africans in the Americas. African slaves had been sailing with European explorers since shortly after Columbus's voyages to the New World. At least thirty slaves accompanied the Spanish explorer Vasco Núñez de Balboa when he discovered the Pacific Ocean in 1513, and Hernán Cortés conquered the Aztec Empire of Mexico in 1521 with a small army of soldiers, sailors, and slaves.

The Spanish adventurer Lucas Vázquez de Ayllón made the first attempt to found a colony including African slaves in North America. In 1526 Ayllón landed with five hundred white colonists and about one hundred black slaves on the coast of what is now South Carolina. The settlers founded the colony of San Miguel de Guadalupe. However, their venture soon ended in disaster. When Ayllón and many of the

Jamestown settlers gather to inspect the African captives brought by a Dutch slave ship.

other settlers died of fever, the survivors fought over the right to lead the colony. Taking advantage of the turmoil, the Africans staged a rebellion and fled into the forests, where they may have taken refuge in a Native American community. In December 1527 the remaining 150 white colonists abandoned San Miguel.

vive. In time, Jamestown became a boomtown, with a thriving economy based on large exports of tobacco to England.

The labor on Jamestown's tobacco plantations was performed by English indentured servants and African slaves. A Dutch trading ship brought the first captive Africans to the settlement in 1619. Colonists soon realized that it was more profitable to enslave black Africans for life than to rely on the temporary labor of white indentured servants. As other British colonies sprang up along the Atlantic coast of North America, slavery put down deep roots in the new American society.

Over time British slave ships would deliver thousands of African captives to the North American colonies. Britain also won the Spanish *asiento,* gaining the exclusive right to import slaves to the Spanish West Indies. In addition, British traders became the main supplier of slave laborers to Dutch and French New World colonies. By the late 1700s, Great Britain was the largest slaving nation in the world, transporting more than half of all captives taken from Africa across the Atlantic Ocean.

COLONIAL AMERICA ENTERS THE SLAVE TRADE

A group of Boston merchants was responsible for colonial America's first attempt to enter the profitable business of importing African slaves. In 1644 the merchants financed the voyage of three slave ships to Africa. One of the American ships completed the trade triangle. It seized captives in West Africa; exchanged them for sugar, tobacco, salt, and wine in Barbados; and carried the trade goods back to Boston. The other two vessels returned empty, after barely escaping well-armed European warships along the African coast. The colonies did not yet have the resources to challenge the European powers that were competing for control of the transatlantic slave trade.

As Britain gained the upper hand in the slave trade, however, the British colonists in North America began to play a more active role. In the early 1700s, slave trading flourished in the north-ern colonies, especially in New England. Some colonial slave traders sailed directly to the West Indies to trade for slaves. Others loaded their ships with goods such as rum and iron bars, which they exchanged for captives in Africa. The African captives were then transported to the West Indies or colonial America for sale. These advertisements for newly imported African cap-tives appeared in northern newspapers in the early 1760s:

Slaves waiting to be sold at a market in Richmond, Virginia. This may be the last time some of these women have with their children, who could be purchased by different owners.

> Just imported from the Coast of Africa, in the Schooner PENELOPE, now lying at Mr. Hughe's Wharff, A PARCEL of likely Negroe Boys and Girls, and to be sold by THOMAS CARPEN-TER, on board said Schooner.

> Just imported in the Sloop Company, Captain Hodgson, from the Coast of Africa, A PARCEL OF LIKELY NEGROE SLAVES; Which may be seen on board said Sloop, lying off Cooper's Ferry.

LAND OF THE "FREE"

Millions of enslaved Africans helped build the "free" society that would eventually become the United States. Many of the founders of the new American republic lived side by side with their slaves, deriving financial benefits and social advantages from the profitable plantation economy. Americans often seemed unaware of the contradictions at the heart of their society. In 1807, for example, an American ship sailed from South Carolina to West Africa, took on 179 captured Africans, and delivered the captives into slavery in Cuba. The ship was named the *Fourth of July*, in honor of America's declaration of freedom and independence from England.

Just imported from the Coast of Africa, in the Brig Nancy, and to be sold at Wilmington, in New Castle County . . . ONE Hundred and Seventy five Gold Coast NEGROES. . . . In the West India Islands, where Slaves are best known, those of the Gold Coast are in much greater Esteem, and higher valued, than any others, on Account of their natural good Dispositions, and being better capable of hard Labour.

By the eve of the American Revolution, slave trading had become the foundation of New England's economy. Countless businesses and industries depended on the trade. These included shipbuilding, fishing, some forms of farming, logging, insurance, law, and the making of rum, sails, barrels, rope, and many other goods. One wealthy tradesman in Newport, Rhode Island, wrote that "an Ethiopian could as soon change his skin as a Newport merchant could be induced to change so lucrative [profitable] a trade as that in slaves for the slow profits of any manufactory."

BLESSING THE TRADE

When Pope Alexander VI issued the decree ordering Spain and Portugal to divide the world between them, he declared that the division would advance the cause of Christianity. Bringing Christian worship to "remote and unknown" regions of the world was the highest of all goals, said the pope. It was "well pleasing" to God that "the Christian religion be exalted and be everywhere increased and spread, . . . and that barbarous nations be overthrown and brought to the faith."

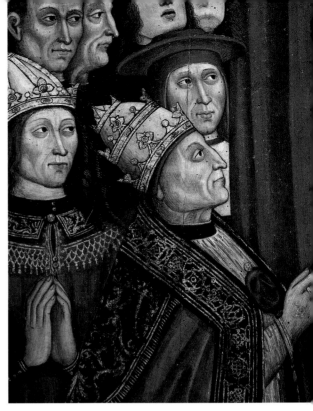

Alexander VI became pope in 1492, the year Columbus reached the Americas. In 1493 he gave the Spanish the right to preach Christianity in all the lands Columbus had visited.

To most Christians in Europe and colonial America, the native peoples of Africa were heathens—uncivilized savages who did not believe in the God of the Bible. Leaders of Christian churches often promoted slavery as a means of saving the souls of these "barbarians" by introducing them to Christianity. Clergymen often blessed slave ships, which might bear names such as *John the Baptist* or *Gift of God*, before the slavers set sail from Africa with their human cargo. In the Americas ministers sometimes blessed and baptized the captives who were put on the auction block. Many religious leaders in both Europe and the Americas were slave owners themselves.

Slave-ship owners and captains often considered themselves devout Christians, too. Captains frequently conducted religious services during their transatlantic crossings. Not surprisingly, these worship services were usually segregated, involving the white seamen only.

The British seaman John Newton swore his devotion to

Christianity after he was saved from drowning during an Atlantic crossing in the mid-1700s. Newton went on to serve as the captain of a slave ship. For several years he enjoyed what he described as "an easy and creditable [respectable] way of life." In time, however, Newton's views on slavery began to change. He left the sea and became a minister and an outspoken opponent of the slave trade. In 1770 he wrote these lyrics for the famous hymn "Amazing Grace":

> Amazing grace, how sweet the sound
> That saved a wretch like me.
> I once was lost, but now am found,
> Was blind, but now I see.

John Newton, the slave-ship captain who became a minister, hymn writer, and campaigner against the slave trade

Some European and colonial Jews were also involved in the transatlantic slave trade. During the early 1600s, Jews who had emigrated from Portugal were the main dealers in African slaves in Brazil. Acting as "middlemen," these merchants bought tens of thousands of captives imported by Dutch slave traders and sold them to Brazilian plantation owners. In other areas of the New World, Jewish merchants played a very small role in the buying and selling of African slaves. One of the best-known Jewish slave traders in colonial North America was Aaron Lopez, a Portuguese immigrant in Newport, Rhode Island. According to some sources, Lopez commissioned fourteen slaving ventures in the 1770s, carrying about one thousand slaves into Rhode Island.

African Participation in the Slave Trade

At the start of the transatlantic slave trade, captives were abducted from communities on the west coast of Africa by small parties of European raiders. Soon Europeans realized that they could acquire slaves more quickly and easily through alliances with African rulers. Many chiefs were glad to exchange their captives for prized European goods such as horses, guns, ammunition, alcohol, and tobacco.

At first, most of the slaves traded by the rulers of West African states and kingdoms were prisoners who had been captured in intertribal wars. As the demand for slaves increased, some chiefs began to wage wars against their neighbors solely for the purpose of taking captives. Rivals for a ruler's power, criminals, and some people falsely accused of crimes were also sold into slavery. Poor families were sometimes forced to sell their children to pay off heavy debts.

African slave traders and raiders also bought or kidnapped millions of men, women, and children from inland villages and marched them to slave trading centers on the coast. In 1788 British ship's surgeon Alexander Falconbridge wrote that he had "great reason to believe that most of the negroes shipped from the coast of Africa are kidnapped. I was told by a negroe woman that as she was on her return home one evening from some neighbours, . . . she was kidnapped and [even though] she was big with child, sold for a slave." In his anti-slavery text *Thoughts and Sentiments on the Evil and Wicked*

Aaron Lopez, an immigrant from Portugal, prospered as a slave trader in Rhode Island.

Slave raids continued in Africa until the late nineteenth century. Raiders might wipe out entire villages, killing everyone they didn't take captive.

Traffic of the Commerce of the Human Species, the former slave Ottobah Cugoano wrote, "I must own, to the shame of my own countrymen, that I was first kidnapped and betrayed by some of my own complexion, who were the first cause of my exile and slavery."

Students of history sometimes ask why Africans sold their own countrymen into slavery. There are many different answers to that question. For one, African slave traders did not believe that they were selling their countrymen but rather people from separate states or kingdoms. Also, and perhaps most importantly, the majority of African traders probably did not realize that they were selling their captives into a different and much harsher system of slavery than the form traditionally practiced in their homeland. Some rulers delivered captives into the hands of European traders in order to prevent raids on their own people. Others were motivated by greed. A chief who sold many captives to the slave traders could quickly grow richer and more powerful than his neighbors.

While it is true that many Africans were deeply involved in slave trading, it was the Europeans who controlled and greatly expanded the trade. In time the people of Africa were caught up in a system beyond their control. The introduction of guns to the African continent increased intertribal rivalries and wars. Africans were forced to arm themselves for protection against neighboring communities; to acquire arms, they had to capture their neighbors and sell them into slavery. Some Africans were forced into the slave trade for protection against the European slave traders. In the nineteenth century, for example, the Ashanti people of Ghana sold slaves to the Portuguese, Spanish, and French in exchange for arms and ammunition. The Ashanti used the weapons to fight off British traders who were trying to take control of their towns and trade routes. It was no use, however; Ghana was eventually conquered and colonized by European forces.

In spite of all the factors compelling Africans to participate in the transatlantic slave trade, there were many who refused. For every chief or trader who profited from the buying and selling of human beings, many other Africans resisted, often at the cost of their own lives.

Gainsborough Pinx.

F. Bartolozzi Sculp.

Chapter 4

The Trade Triangle

IN 1729 A COUPLE LOOKING FORWARD TO THE BIRTH OF their first child was captured in Guinea, West Africa, and sold to European slave traders. The child, a boy, was born in the hold of a slave ship as it crossed the Atlantic Ocean. By the time the ship docked in South America two months later, both parents were dead. A priest baptized the orphaned child, naming him Ignatius. At age two the little boy was taken to England. There he worked as a child slave in the home of three sisters who renamed him Sancho. In time Ignatius Sancho won his freedom and went on to become a well-known writer and composer.

Ignatius Sancho was just one of millions of Africans caught up in the three-sided trading pattern known as the trade triangle. Altogether, the trade triangle was about ten thousand miles long, depending on the exact destinations on each leg of the

Ignatius Sancho was born in the hold of a slave ship but died as a free man and well-known writer in 1780.

journey. For a rough idea of that distance, imagine traveling from the east coast of the United States to the west coast, then back to the east coast, then back once again. To make the complete circuit of the trade triangle could take anywhere from one to several years.

THE FIRST LEG: FROM EUROPE TO AFRICA

Europeans who traveled to West Africa for trade gave names to various sections of the coast, reflecting the types of goods commonly obtained there. Traders spoke of the Gold Coast, the Ivory Coast, the Grain Coast, and the Pepper Coast. As the buying and selling of human beings became more profitable than any other form of trade, they began to refer to hundreds of miles along the coast of West Africa as simply the Slave Coast.

The crew of a ship sailing from Europe to the Slave Coast included the captain and several other officers, gunners to handle the ship's cannons, a doctor (known as the ship's surgeon), a carpenter, a cook, a blacksmith, a sailmaker, and several additional seamen. Captains usually engaged extra crew members, in anticipation of losing a certain number to death or desertion during the voyage. Many of those who signed up for the difficult, dangerous life on a slave ship were fleeing from debts or imprisonment. Some men were "shanghaied," or forced aboard with the help of liquor, drugs, or a club, in order to fill out the crew. In the mid-1700s slave-ship captain John Newton described his crew as "the refuse and dregs of the nation, . . . boys impatient of their parents or masters, or already ruined by some untimely vice and for the most part devoid of all good principles."

Slave ships sailed from Europe loaded with manufactured goods, including iron and copper bars, colored glass beads,

THE THREE SIDES OF THE TRADE TRIANGLE

Trade triangle is a simplified term that is used for an assortment of complicated transactions. The "typical" triangular trading voyage involved these three stages:

Side One: Ships carrying manufactured goods sailed from Spain, Portugal, Great Britain, France, Belgium, the Netherlands, and other European nations to the west coast of Africa.

Side Two (the Middle Passage): Ships sailed from Africa across the Atlantic Ocean to the Americas, carrying African captives and raw materials such as gold.

Side Three: Ships sailed back to Europe, loaded with goods produced on plantations in the Americas.

Not all ships involved in the transatlantic slave trade made the three-stage journey. Some slaving voyages involved more than three exchanges of trade goods. Some involved only two passages, with ships sailing back and forth between Europe and Africa or the Americas and Africa. In addition, beginning in the eighteenth century, an increasing number of slave ships began and ended their voyages in colonial America. Whatever the exact process, all these ventures in some way involved the exchange of human beings for trade goods.

brass and pewter utensils, textiles, tobacco, wine, brandy, rum, swords, guns, and ammunition. When a ship reached the West African coast, the captain exchanged his cargo for slaves. Europeans also might trade their merchandise for raw materials such as grain, ivory, gold, and animal hides.

Slave trading between Europeans and Africans was a long, complicated process. The ship's captain and officers were eager to get as many healthy captives as possible for their merchandise. The African chief and his counselors were also determined to earn the greatest possible profit. An elaborate ritual of gifts and entertaining, dining and drinking, arguments and compliments surrounded the bargaining sessions. Negotiations might stretch over hours or even days until the two sides agreed to exchange a certain quantity of goods for a certain number of captives. The final agreements were often incredibly complex. In a typical transaction, "a man and a fine girl" were exchanged for "one roll tobacco, one . . . pipe coral, one gun, three cutlasses [swords], one brass blunderbuss [short-barreled musket], twenty-four linen handkerchiefs, 5 patches, 3 jugs rum, . . . 12 pint mugs, one laced hat, one linen handkerchief."

The captain and crew of the slave ship were paid by the "head," or the number of slaves delivered. That meant that leaving Africa with empty cargo space was bad business. In the early days of the slave trade, slavers might cruise along the African coast for a few weeks or as long as several months, stopping now and then to bargain for captives. The longer a ship remained in Africa, the more crew members it risked losing. Sailors sickened and died from the heat, humidity, and tropical diseases such as yellow fever and malaria, transmitted by infected mosquitoes. At the end of the eighteenth century, the death rate for European sailors in Africa was one in five. The Guinea Coast, a region spanning present-day Benin, Nigeria, Cameroon, and Guinea, was known as the "white man's grave." A popular seaman's rhyme warned, "Beware and take heed of the Bight of Benin, where few come out though many go in."

As time went by, traders found ways to reduce their risks by speeding up the delivery of slaves. African chiefs and slave raiders brought their captives to European forts or slave warehouses along the coast, where the prisoners were collected and held for shipment. One of the most important of the slave warehouses was on Gorée Island, off the coast of Senegal. An estimated 20 million Africans were imprisoned on Gorée Island between the mid-1500s and mid-1800s, awaiting the ships of Dutch, English, or French slave traders. About 6 million died without ever leaving the island.

The conditions in the warehouse at Gorée Island were appalling. Men, women, and children bound with chains and shackles were crammed in a filthy dungeon, with as many as thirty people to each eight-foot-square cell. The captives were fed and allowed to relieve themselves once a day. Meanwhile, on the floors above their heads, European officers and slave traders lived in relative luxury. Stanislas-Jean de Boufflers, a French aristo-

Gorée Island, the "point of no return" for millions of captive Africans, seen from the coast of Senegal

Captives were taken to the slave ships through this tunnel on Gorée Island.

crat who served as governor of Gorée Island in the late 1700s, was known for his lavish dinner parties and receptions. However, Boufflers complained that the Europeans living on the upper floors of the governor's residence had to endure "the stench of the corpses of the captives who die in their dozens in the dungeons and which the traders, in order to economize, throw in the water with cannonballs attached to their feet."

THE MIDDLE PASSAGE: FROM AFRICA TO THE AMERICAS

Before slave ships began their grueling voyage from Africa to the Americas, the captives were loaded into the ship's windowless cargo hold. Ships were also loaded with supplies for the long Atlantic crossing. These essential goods included wood for cooking, barrels of drinking water, and food for the crew and captives. The records of a slave ship that carried 250 captives contained this list of food provisions:

17,000 pounds of small beans
50,000 yams
11 pigs
12 coops of fowl and ducks
dried beef and fish
rice, millet seed, farina, and macaroni
raisins and almonds
wine and ales

An Atlantic crossing generally took from four to fourteen weeks. A number of factors could affect that timetable, including the weather, winds, ocean currents, and the design and condition of the slave ship. As the ship made its way across the seas, the Africans in the hold endured unimaginable horrors. Life above deck was also perilous. The sailors worked long hours on limited food and water. When the ship was crowded with goods and supplies, they slept out on the open deck. Some died from injury or disease. The medical knowledge of the time was limited, and infectious diseases spread quickly through the crowded, unsanitary ships. Others died in battles with enemy ships or pirates. Still other sailors perished in storms. "Suddenly the weather closes in," recalled a seaman from Brazil, "and the seas rise so high and so strongly that the ships must obey the waves, sailing at the mercy of the winds without true course or control. . . . One ship or another will break apart from the fury of the storm, and sink. Another drifts on, dismasted, its rigging ruined by the will of the ocean, . . . on the verge of capsizing."

Seamen also suffered from the harsh discipline commonly practiced by slave-ship commanders. British ship's surgeon Alexander Falconbridge observed that "most of the sailors were treated with brutal severity. . . . A young man on board one of the ships was frequently beaten in a very severe manner, for very trifling faults. This was done sometimes with what is termed a cat [a whip with nine 'tails'] and sometimes he was beaten with a bamboo."

The sailors who made it through the long, harrowing Middle Passage shouted with joy at their first sight of

A ship's officer, holding a cat-o'-nine-tails, kicks a slave. The "cat" was used to punish disobedient sailors as well as to intimidate slaves.

the green lands of the Americas. There the Africans who had survived the journey were unloaded and sold. Slave-ship captains usually sold their captives directly to plantation owners at an agreed-upon price. Slaves might also go to the highest bidders at slave auctions, or they might be sold at noisy, frenzied gatherings known as "scrambles." Alexander Falconbridge described one scramble that took place in the West Indies. After agreeing to sell all his captives at the same price, the captain herded them into a large yard. The gates were opened, and a mob of buyers rushed in.

> Some instantly seized such of the Negroes as they could conveniently lay hold of with their hands. Others being prepared with several handkerchiefs tied together, encircled as many as they were able. . . . It is scarcely possible to describe the confusion. . . . The poor astonished Negroes were so terrified by these proceedings, that several of them, through fear climbed over the walls of the courtyard and ran wild about the town, but were soon hunted down and retaken.

With the proceeds from the sale of their captives, slave-ship captains bought goods that had been produced by the enslaved Africans already on the plantations. Besides sugar, the most valued New World product, slave traders might buy tobacco, coffee, rum, molasses, rice, spices, indigo, wood, and products made from the palm tree, including oil, wax, fiber, and medicines. All this cargo was packed into the ship's empty holds, where the slaves had been kept.

The Last Leg: From the Americas to Europe

After slave ships were loaded with their new cargo and supplies, they set sail on the final leg of their triangular journey. The passage from the Americas to Europe, like that from Africa to the New World, could take from four to fourteen weeks. Often a few slaves who had not been sold in the colonies returned with the ship to Europe. These captives usually belonged to the captain, who planned to sell them through newspaper advertisements or slave auctions. Some of these people might work as seamen, replacing crew members who had died or deserted.

By the time the slave ship reached Europe and completed its long triangular trading journey, hundreds of people—including many who had never set foot on board—had shared in the profits. Slave traders in Africa had been paid for their captives. Plantation owners in the Americas had earned profits on the sale of their goods and added workers to their labor force. The captain and crew of the slave ship had been rewarded with a commission based on the number of slaves delivered alive. The investors who had financed the voyage earned a return from the sale of the slaves and trade goods. Banks and insurance companies collected their fees from shipowners, and the many businesses connected with the slave trade benefited from the sale of their goods and services. Even ordinary Europeans and Americans might sample the riches of the slave trade, by purchasing shares in slaving voyages, in the hope that their "ship would come in." Everyone involved in the many transactions of the transatlantic slave trade profited—everyone, that is, except the slaves.

Chapter 5

DOWN IN THE HOLD

IN 1698 A MERCHANT SHIP CALLED THE *HENRIETTA MARIE* completed its first slave-trading voyage. The small, sturdy ship had sailed the trade triangle, traveling from London to the Guinea region of West Africa, on to the West Indies, then back to London. According to shipping records, the voyage had been a great success. The captain had sold "250 Negro slaves and 105 Elephants Teeth [tusks]" at a good price in Barbados, and he brought home a valuable cargo of sugar.

While the *Henrietta Marie* sat in the port of London, workers prepared it for its next voyage. They swabbed the wooden decks, repaired the canvas sails on the three tall masts, and polished the eight cast-iron cannons. They also added something new. When the ship next set sail for Africa, it had a handsome bronze bell to toll the hours for sailors on watch. Nearly three centuries later, that bell would provide the answer to a mystery.

The *Henrietta Marie*, a seventeenth-century merchant vessel used in the slave trade

THE TERRIBLE CROSSING

There was no such thing as a "typical" slave ship. Any vessel suited for carrying cargo could be used to transport captive

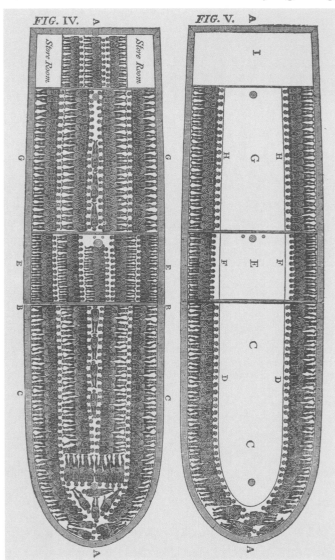

human beings. Small slave ships might hold up to 250 captives, while larger ships could carry 600 or more. Slave traders debated the best way to pack their human cargo. Captains who were "tight packers" crammed in as many slaves as possible, hoping that the extra numbers would make up for captives who died during the crossing. "Loose packers" allowed a little more space, as well as slightly more food and exercise. They believed that better treatment meant more survivors, which in turn meant a higher cash return at the journey's end.

Captive Africans were transported belowdecks, in the ship's cargo hold. The holds of slave ships were usually fitted with layers of flat shelves, on which men, women, and children were stored like spoons in a drawer. The captives lay in a low

This diagram shows how African captives were "stowed" in the holds of an English slave ship in 1791.

coffinlike space, chained together by their hands and feet, unable to stand or sit. The air was stifling, and the heat and odors were nearly unbearable. Olaudah Equiano, an African transported into slavery in the mid-1700s, later wrote that the "loathsomeness of the stench . . . the closeness of the place, and the heat of the climate, added to the number in the ship, which was so crowded that each had scarcely room to turn himself, almost suffocated us." (For more on Olaudah Equiano, see the first book in this series, *Africa: A Look Back.*)

Twice a day the captives in the hold were given water and a meal of yams, beans, or rice and sometimes a little dried beef or pork. To cover up the foul taste of boiled horsebeans or spoiled meat, the food might be coated with a mixture of flour, water, pepper, and palm oil known as "slabber sauce." The captives were forced to relieve themselves where they lay or, if space allowed, in buckets.

Enslaved Africans endured these nightmarish conditions for the duration of the Middle Passage, which could take up to fourteen weeks. Many captives went mad or sank into misery and despair. Some tried to escape their torment by starving themselves. The crew force-fed these desperate people by prying their jaws open and pouring food down their throats. After a voyage in 1693, slave ship captain Thomas Phillips reported that "about twelve Negroes did wilfully drown themselves, and others starved themselves to death."

Captive Africans also sickened and died in the filthy, crowded, rat-infested cargo holds. According to Captain Phillips, sharks sometimes followed slave ships all the way from Africa to the Americas "for the dead Negroes that are thrown overboard in the passage." Ruthless captains sometimes threw sick captives alive into the sea to keep them from infecting the rest of the ship. In 1781 the captain of the British slave ship *Zong* ordered his crew to throw 133 sick slaves overboard as the ship drew near the Caribbean islands. According to one of the sailors, the captain explained that, under the law,

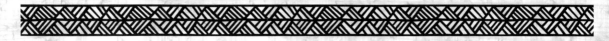

"DANCING THE SLAVES"

Many slave-ship captains swore that the best way to ensure the health of enslaved Africans was to make them dance. Once a day the crew led the captives up on deck and forced them to jump around in their iron shackles. Music might be provided by a sailor playing a fiddle or bagpipe or a slave pounding on a drum or upside-down kettle. Even the sick and injured were forced to dance. Captives who did not move quickly enough to suit their overseers were "encouraged" with a smack of the cat-o'-nine-tails.

One ship's captain observed that his human merchandise "jumped to the lash so promptly that there was not much occasion for scoring [cutting] their naked flanks." It was satisfying, he wrote, to know that "these pleasant exercises were keeping our stock in good condition and, of course, enhancing our prospects of making a profitable voyage." The captives' view of the humiliating and painful practice of "dancing the slaves" was expressed in a poem by an African woman known as Yamba:

At the savage Captain's beck
Now like Brutes they make us prance
Smack the Cat about the Deck
And in scorn they bid us dance.

Above: Crewmen with whips taunt three slaves and force them to dance.

the ship's owners would bear the cost of any slaves who died of disease, but "if they were thrown overboard alive into the sea, it would be the loss of the underwriters [insurance company]."

DESPERATE CARGO

Despite their fear, hunger, sickness, chains, and the difficulty of communicating with fellow captives who spoke many different languages, Africans on slave ships often fought back against their captors. There are at least three hundred documented cases of shipboard slave mutinies. Many others probably went unrecorded. Two of the best-known revolts took place on the slave ships *Creole* and *Amistad.*

The *Creole* was an American ship that sailed from Virginia in October 1841, carrying 135 captive men, women, and children to a slave market in New Orleans. As the ship passed near Nassau, a British territory in the Bahamas, a captive known as Madison Washington led a band of eighteen Africans in a mutiny. The rebels seized control of the ship and forced one of the crewmen to sail it into Nassau. There a court ruled that, under an 1833 British law abolishing slavery throughout the British Empire, the *Creole* slaves were free. That ruling enraged American plantation owners and government officials, who demanded that the slaves be returned to their "rightful owners." The British government refused, but the slaveholders were eventually awarded $110,330 to cover the cost of their lost "property."

The *Amistad* was a small black schooner outfitted for coastal slave trading. In 1839 the ship was transporting fifty-three captive Africans on the last leg of a long voyage into slavery. Most of the captives had been seized by raiders in the African interior

A man rebelling against his enslavement prepares to defend himself.

and sold to Spanish slave traders. They had been transported across the Atlantic to Havana, Cuba, where they were purchased by sugar planters. The *Amistad* was carrying the Africans along the coast to the plantations. On their third night at sea, a young man known as Cinque used a nail to free himself and several other captives from their irons. Arming themselves with long-handled sugarcane knives, the mutineers seized control of the ship, killing the captain and three crewmen.

Under Cinque's leadership, the Africans ordered two of the remaining seamen to sail the *Amistad* back to Africa. Instead, the sailors followed a wandering course that brought the vessel to the shores of the United States. The U.S. navy captured the *Amistad* off the coast of Long Island, New York. The Africans were imprisoned for murder and piracy. Their trials attracted national attention, with thousands of Americans eagerly following the legal debate over slavery, liberty, and property rights. Finally, former president John Quincy Adams presented their case before the U.S. Supreme Court. The justices ruled that the Africans had been illegally enslaved and therefore had the right to fight for their freedom. Nearly three years after the start of their long ordeal, the thirty-five surviving *Amistad* captives returned to Africa.

Not all slave mutinies ended as successfully as the incidents on the *Creole* and *Amistad*. Captives who took part in failed mutinies were usually punished swiftly and brutally. While Ottobah Cugoano was crossing the Atlantic in the 1750s, he and his fellow captives decided that "death was more preferable than life" and devised a plan to "burn and blow up the ship, and to perish all together in the flames." After the plan was discovered, wrote Cugoano, there was "a cruel bloody scene."

John Atkins, a sailor serving on the British slave ship *Robert* in 1721, described what happened after another attempted slave mutiny. After the mutineers were overcome by crewmen armed with muskets, the ship's captain decided to spare the lives of the two strong ringleaders, because he hoped to sell them for a good price. He tortured and killed four less valuable mutineers, however, including a woman who had helped in the revolt. She was "hoisted up by the Thumbs," wrote Atkins, "whipp'd, and slashed . . . with Knives before the other Slaves till she died."

The Wreck of the *Henrietta Marie*

In September 1699 the *Henrietta Marie* left London on its second slave-trading voyage. Two months later, the ship sailed from West Africa with a cargo of about 250 captive Africans. The men, women, and children were chained together in the ship's stifling cargo hold. Sixty captives died during the fourteen-week Atlantic crossing. As the ship drew near Jamaica, the 190 survivors were brought up on deck to prepare them for market. They were bathed and their skin was rubbed with palm oil to make their sores and wounds less visible. Their food rations were increased to make them look stronger and healthier.

In Jamaica the captives from the *Henrietta Marie* were sold to plantation owners at a slave auction. The hold of the ship was packed with sugar, indigo, cotton, and other trade goods. In June 1700 the heavily laden vessel set sail for its home port of London. Historians believe that the *Henrietta Marie* ran into a hurricane in the Florida Straits. The ship sank thirty-seven miles west of Key West, Florida, along with its crew of about eighteen seamen.

Nearly three hundred years later, divers discovered the remains of an unidentified ship on a shallow coral reef off Florida's coast. Moe Molinar, an African-American deep-sea diver, investigated the site. Running his hands over the sandy ocean floor, Molinar felt something cold and solid. He dug up a chunk of heavy iron handcuffs. "I knew right away what they were and what they were used for," he recalled. "It hit me, like someone hitting me in the head. I was holding shackles that had bound the wrists and legs of black people who had been brought here as slaves."

Divers eventually brought up thousands of artifacts from the unidentified shipwreck. They found more than one hundred iron shackles, including large cuffs designed for the wrists and ankles of men and smaller ones for women and children. Other recovered items included elephant tusks, copper cooking vessels, pewter spoons and jugs, glass beads, muskets, cannons, and cannonballs. But the most important find was the ship's heavy bronze bell. When divers chipped away the crust of limestone and coral covering the bell, they saw an inscription: THE HENRIETTA MARIE 1699. With that discovery they realized that they had found the earliest known slave-ship wreck.

Today the *Henrietta Marie* is the world's largest source of

The underwater plaque commemorating the *Henrietta Marie* and the slaves who were transported on this and countless other ships

objects from the early years of the slave trade. The remains of its last voyage have given historians a wealth of information about the transatlantic slave trade. A traveling exhibit of artifacts from the sunken ship has also given thousands of Americans a greater understanding of the hardships endured by enslaved Africans in the Middle Passage.

In 1993 a group of African-American scuba divers placed a memorial plaque underwater at the site of the *Henrietta Marie*. The bronze marker bears the ship's name and this message:

IN MEMORY AND RECOGNITION OF THE COURAGE,

PAIN AND SUFFERING OF ENSLAVED AFRICAN PEOPLE.

SPEAK HER NAME AND GENTLY TOUCH

THE SOULS OF OUR ANCESTORS.

Chapter 6

ABOLISHING THE TRANSATLANTIC SLAVE TRADE

THE END OF THE TRANSATLANTIC SLAVE TRADE AND the end of slavery were two very different events. Putting an end to the importing of newly enslaved Africans was the first step toward abolishing slavery in Europe and the United States. But the institution of slavery had become central to the economy and society in many nations. It would not be easy to abolish a way of life that depended on the labor of millions of captive black men, women, and children. At the start of the eighteenth century, abolition was in the air, but it was still just a whisper.

THE BEGINNING OF THE END

The strongest resistance to ending the slave trade came from the people who had profited the most from plantations in the Americas and from related businesses in both the Americas

A British patrol boat intercepts an illegal slave ship after the abolition of the transatlantic slave trade.

THE COTTON GIN

Some of the advances of the Industrial Revolution strengthened rather than weakened the institution of slavery. The most important of these innovations was the cotton gin, patented by American inventor Eli Whitney in 1794. The cotton gin greatly speeded up the process of cleaning harvested cotton. That made it profitable for farmers in the southern and western United States to grow cotton. More and more slaves were transported from Africa to the United States to work on the cotton plantations. You'll find more information on the cotton gin and the growth of slavery in nineteenth-century America in the third book in this series, *Slavery and Resistance.*

and Europe. These supporters of slavery argued that their nations' economies would collapse without a consistent supply of slave labor. Slaveholders also continued to insist that slavery was a positive institution, because it offered the "inferior" black race the benefits of Christianity and Western civilization. Meanwhile, for the majority of non-slaveholding Americans and Europeans, the slave trade seemed a remote and unimportant topic. While such people often benefited from the products of slavery, they knew little about its horrors.

Despite all these obstacles, the movement toward abolition was growing. One factor contributing to this trend was the Industrial Revolution. The Industrial Revolution began in Britain in the late eighteenth century and soon spread to other European countries and to the United States. These nations shifted from an economy based on agriculture to one based on the mass production of manufactured goods.

While the causes of the Industrial Revolution were complex, one of its main features was the introduction of many new types of power-driven machinery. James Watt's improved steam engine, developed in 1769, made it possible for machines to perform work more quickly and efficiently than had previously been done by hand. The spinning jenny, patented by James Hargreaves in 1770, automated the production of cotton thread. The power loom, introduced by Edmund Cartwright in 1785, speeded up the weaving of cotton cloth. These and other inventions reduced the cost of manufacturing goods. That made it less profitable to transport African laborers to Europe and the Americas. Instead, industries began to rely on free wage earners or on slaves born within the country.

Another factor that contributed to the decline of the slave trade was the Haitian Revolution. In August 1791 thousands of Haitian slaves armed with knives and torches rose against their French colonial masters. They set fire to plantations and slaughtered more than a thousand white men, women, and children. Over the next thirteen years, French and British forces battled unsuccessfully to regain control of the colony. By 1804, the revolutionaries had driven out the Europeans, freed all the slaves, and founded the world's first independent black republic. The bloody Haitian Revolution terrified white slaveholders throughout the Atlantic region. One visitor touring the southern United States observed that slave owners "cannot go to bed in the evening without the

Toussaint L'Ouverture (standing, in the center), Haiti's first national hero, leads slaves in rebellion against their French masters.

apprehension [fear] of being massacred before morning!" The fear of slave rebellions would become one of the main reasons cited by American and British lawmakers for restricting the transatlantic slave trade.

Another very important factor leading to the abolition of the slave trade was a growing public awareness of the horrors of slavery. In the late eighteenth century, abolitionists in Europe and North America launched wide-reaching campaigns to arouse antislavery sentiments. Leaders of the abolition movement wrote articles, distributed pamphlets, and gave speeches describing the horrible conditions aboard slave ships. They petitioned legislators to abolish the trade, calling on their sense of humanity, justice, and Christian morality.

One of the leaders of the British antislavery campaign was William Wilberforce, a social reformer who served in Parliament for forty years. In 1789 Wilberforce gave an emotional speech to fellow lawmakers, announcing that he had thoroughly investigated the slave trade. "So enormous, so dreadful, so irremediable [incurable] did its wickedness appear," he declared, "that my own mind was completely made up for the abolition." Wilberforce pledged to introduce a new bill to abolish the slave trade every year until he succeeded in getting the legislation passed.

Former slaves were among the most impassioned voices raised against the slave trade. Slave narratives published by abolitionist presses introduced white readers not only to the brutality of the slave system but also to the humanity of enslaved Africans—for the first time, they could be seen as fellow human

This portrait of William Wilberforce was painted when he was twenty-nine, the year before he made his famous speech in Parliament. Wilberforce was devoted to the antislavery cause for the rest of his life.

beings. One of the most important of these autobiographical tales was *The Interesting Narrative of the Life of Olaudah Equiano,* written in 1789. (For more on slave narratives, see the first book in this series, *Africa: A Look Back.*)

Banning the Trade

Great Britain, the country that had dominated transatlantic slave trading in the late eighteenth century, was also the first European nation to ban it. In 1807 the British Parliament passed the Abolition of the Slave Trade Act. The law made it illegal for any British subject to capture or transport slaves.

After the British banned the slave trade, they began to pressure other European nations to follow their lead. By 1820, France, Spain, the Netherlands, Sweden, Russia, and Austria had all agreed to pass laws prohibiting the importing of African slaves. The last major holdout was Portugal. The European

Abolitionists in an English city celebrate the end of their nation's slave trade.

nation that had been the first to engage in the transatlantic slave trade finally outlawed the practice in 1830.

In colonial America the international slave trade came to a standstill during the American Revolution. That temporary halt was caused mainly by economic factors. At the same time, there were many Americans who were troubled by the contradictions of fighting a war for freedom while 20 percent of the nation was enslaved.

After the war's end, the Constitutional Convention met in Philadelphia to draft the U.S. Constitution. Delegates to the convention heatedly debated the controversial issues of slavery and the slave trade. Slavery was dying out in the North, where most colonies would soon vote for its gradual or immediate abolition. In the South, however, plantations producing cotton, tobacco, and other crops were the backbone of the economy, and those vast estates depended on a large slave labor force. After long negotiations, the delegates agreed to a compromise. The Constitution adopted in September 1787 contained a clause prohibiting the U.S. Congress from abolishing the slave trade for a period of twenty years. At the end of that period, Congress passed the Act to Prohibit the Importation of Slaves. The law took effect on January 1, 1808, officially ending America's participation in the transatlantic slave trade.

SLAVE SMUGGLING
Even after lawmakers in Europe and the United States abolished the transatlantic slave trade, slavery continued. While the importing of African slaves had been outlawed, owning slaves and buying and selling them within a country were still legal. International slave trading also continued after it was formally

abolished. The price of slaves in the West Indies and other markets had soared with the end of legal trading, and that encouraged slave smugglers to risk penalties in the hope of substantial profits.

Great Britain attempted to combat slave smuggling, but its patrol squadrons could not possibly guard all

Malnourished captives rescued from an illegal slaver

the miles of coastline and open sea. Between 1807 and 1860, the British seized about 1,600 slave ships, freeing 150,000 captive Africans. In that same period, more than 3 million Africans were illegally transported to the Americas. About 250,000 of these were smuggled into the United States.

While many nations allowed British patrols to search their ships for slaves, the United States refused. In addition, Congress did not strongly enforce its own anti–slave trade laws. When U.S. patrols captured a slave ship, they usually turned over the captives to the local government. The result was that Africans seized off the coast of southern slaveholding states could still be sold and enslaved.

In the early 1840s, the United States signed a treaty agreeing to cooperate with Britain in combating slave smuggling. Gradually the combined efforts of Americans and Europeans to halt the illegal transatlantic slave trade began to produce results. Slave smuggling slowed to a trickle. It finally ended in 1888, when Brazil became the last nation in the Western Hemisphere to free its slaves.

Chapter 7

THE IMPACT OF THE SLAVE TRADE

IT IS DIFFICULT TO GRASP THE FULL IMPACT OF THE transatlantic slave trade. The legacy of the brutal forced migration of millions of Africans is woven in many complex ways into the fabric of our modern society. In the United States, slavery's lingering impact can be found in the words we speak, the foods we eat, how we worship, what we see when we look in the mirror, and how we relate to one another.

LINGERING HARMS

For African Americans, many of the harmful effects of the slave trade have persisted from generation to generation. Each act of enslavement broke a link between the slave and his or her culture. Social structures such as family and marriage were damaged through the separation of parents and children, husbands

One result of the forced migration of Africans to the Americas was a lively mixing of cultures. Here a Caribbean couple in Western dress dances to music inspired by their African roots.

and wives. African-based educational systems and traditional rites of passage into adulthood and the community were denied to captives taken far from their homes. Enslaved Africans were even deprived of their names. Captives held at Gorée Island, for example, had their names replaced with numbers. They remained just numbers until they arrived in the New World and were given Portuguese, Spanish, French, or English names. Today some descendants of displaced Africans are still piecing together their identities, searching through old records and stories to find their family ancestors.

One of the most harmful effects of the slave trade was its influence on the minds of slaves and enslavers. White Europeans and Americans adopted many false notions to justify the enslavement of African men, women, and children. Foremost among these was the idea that blacks were inferior beings in need of the control and guidance of the more "civilized" white race. Racist myths persisted even after slavery's end, leading to inequality and injustice. In the United States, racism resulted in discrimination, segregation, and laws that violated the civil rights of African Americans. Today race-based prejudice continues to infect our society and poison relations between black and white Americans.

The mentality of the slave years also left some African Americans with a lingering sense of shame and inferiority. Sociologists believe that many of the problems that have plagued black communities can be traced back to patterns of behavior established during the slave trade. Those problems include poverty, lower educational levels, and a higher incidence of broken families. Clearly the wounds left by centuries of slavery have still not completely healed.

This exhibit in the Kura Holanda Slave Museum on the Caribbean island of Curacao expresses both the lasting pain inflicted by slavery and the determination of the slaves' descendants to leap free from the legacy of oppression.

THE SCRAMBLE FOR AFRICA

A major political impact of the transatlantic slave trade was the colonization of Africa. The slave-trading nations of Europe reaped huge economic benefits from the buying and selling of Africans and from the crops raised through slave labor on New World plantations. Their strong economies gave them even more power over less developed African states. Europeans who had once been content to trade with African rulers began to hunger for complete domination.

In 1884 representatives from every European nation and the United States met at the Berlin Conference to settle disputes over land claims in Africa. The delegates agreed to divide up the continent for further occupation. While many Africans resisted colonization, they were no match for the well-armed armies of the European powers. By 1905, most of the African continent had become a patchwork of colonies ruled by Great Britain, France, Germany, Belgium, Italy, and Portugal. It would be nearly a century before the peoples of Africa regained their independence.

HARVEST OF THE SLAVE TRADE

As we reflect on the harsh legacy of the transatlantic slave trade, we must also keep in mind the contributions made by enslaved Africans and their descendants. Africans transported to Europe and the Americas brought their diverse cultures with them. Some of the elements of those cultures included traditional belief systems and ways of worship, foods and forms of agriculture, healing techniques, music, dance, art, language, and literature. Africans adapted their beliefs and practices to their new homes, enriching the social and cultural environment around them. In this way, observed historian Stephen D. Behrendt, even "with all of its horrors and inhumanity, the transatlantic slave trade was critical in the formation of the modern world."

For decades the contributions of enslaved Africans and their descendants were largely ignored. Today they are a focus of worldwide attention. Many schools and universities offer courses in African-American studies. Books and films exploring the slave trade and slavery reach an ever-growing audience. One of the most popular authors in the United States, Toni Morrison, has written several best-selling novels about the legacy of slavery and the black American experience. In 1993 Morrison became the first African American to win the Nobel Prize for Literature.

Museums and tourist attractions also offer new insights into the experiences of enslaved Africans. Visitors to the Mel Fisher Maritime Museum in Key West, Florida, can examine slave shackles and other artifacts from the slave ship *Henrietta Marie.* Volunteers in Boston can join the crew of a sailing replica of the *Amistad.* In New York City, tourists can visit the African Burial Ground, a historic cemetery discovered by construction crews digging the foundation for a new office building in 1991. Dating back to the early 1700s, the African Burial Ground holds the remains of an estimated ten thousand to twenty thousand enslaved Africans.

Tourists in African countries can explore some of the sites where the journey into slavery began for millions of Africans. In places such as Elmina Castle in Ghana and Gorée Island off the coast of Senegal, visitors can stand in the dungeons where captives awaited the ships that would take them from their homes forever. Gorée Island, where an estimated 20 million Africans were imprisoned, has become especially important to African-American visitors tracing their roots back to the slave trade.

President and Mrs. Clinton have been among the many visitors to Gorée Island to honor the memory of the African captives who passed through this Door of No Return into a life of slavery.

THE LIVING LEGACY

The slave trade also resulted in new ethnic and social groups. One of these mixed groups is known as the Black Indians. When slaves escaped from their white masters in North America, Native American communities sometimes provided them with shelter

and guidance. Today tens of thousands of Black Indians can trace their heritage to both African and Native American ancestors.

Another mixed community is the Creoles. The term *Creole* originally referred to a white person with French and Spanish roots who settled in the area of New Orleans, Louisiana. As enslaved Africans and their descendants intermingled with the Creoles, the group came to include persons of mixed French or Spanish and African descent. Today many Creoles speak a language, also known as Creole, that developed from a form of French spoken by African slaves in southern Louisiana.

The largest ethnic group that grew out of the slave trade was the African Americans. Africans born in colonial America in the 1600s, slave or free, were the first generation of African Americans. Today the United States is home to an estimated 38.7 million African Americans, whose ancestors include Africans and sometimes Europeans, too.

The African Americans and other descendants of enslaved Africans are the greatest legacy of the transatlantic slave trade. An estimated 10 million to 20 million people survived the Middle Passage, bringing their unique strengths and gifts, along with their memory of tragic losses, to their new homes. Today the children of Africa scattered across the world number more than one billion. Despite the terrible ordeal suffered by their ancestors, they are reclaiming their true history and lost traditions. Their example teaches us about survival, hope, and the triumph of freedom.

Glossary

abolitionist Someone who favored putting an end to slavery.

artifacts Objects from a particular period of history, especially items produced by people.

asiento A contract awarded by Spain to foreign slave traders, granting them the exclusive right to buy slaves in Africa for sale to Spanish colonies in the New World.

bight A bend in a coast that forms a bay of water open to the sea.

cat-o'-nine-tails A whip made from nine knotted cords attached to a handle.

chattel slavery A system in which a slave was legally owned by the slaveholder.

Gold Coast A section of the west coast of Africa around the area of present-day Ghana; Europeans named the region for the large quantities of gold discovered and traded there.

heathens People who do not believe in the God of the Bible. Europeans and colonial Americans used *heathen* as a negative term for Africans and Native Americans.

horsebeans The large flat seeds of the broad-bean plant, which were often used as animal feed; also called fava beans.

indentured servant A person who contracted to work without pay for a specified number of years, often in return for transportation to the New World and essentials such as food, clothes, and housing.

Industrial Revolution An economic and social change that took place at different times in different countries, involving the shift from an economy based on agriculture to one based on the mass production of manufactured goods.

patent An official document granting a special right or privilege.

plantations Large farm estates.

schooner A small two-masted sailing ship.

slave factories Primitive holding pens where captive Africans were collected and held for transport across the Atlantic; also known as "slave warehouses."

slaver A ship used in the slave trade.

sociologists Scientists who study social relationships and institutions.

To Find Out More

BOOKS

Anderson, S. E. *The Black Holocaust for Beginners.* New York: Writers and
    Readers Publishing, 1995.

Cottman, Michael H. *The Wreck of the* Henrietta Marie. New York: Harmony,
    1999.

Feelings, Tom. *The Middle Passage: White Ships, Black Cargo.* New York: Dial
    Books, 1995.

Keller, Kristin Thoennes. *The Slave Trade in Early America.* Mankato, MN:
    Capstone Press, 2004.

VIDEO AND CD-ROM

Africans in America: America's Journey through Slavery. Part 1, *The Terrible
    Transformation, 1450–1750.* VHS. Boston: WGBH Boston Video, 1998.

Eltis, David, Stephen D. Behrendt, David Richardson, and Herbert S. Klein.
    The Transatlantic Slave Trade. CD-ROM. New York: Cambridge Univer-
    sity Press, 2000.

WEB SITES

Africans in America: The Terrible Transformation. WGBH Interactive and PBS
    Online. Copyright © 1998, 1999 WGBH Educational Foundation.
    http://www.pbs.org/wgbh/aia/part1/1narr3.html

The Atlantic Slave Trade and Slave Life in the Americas: A Visual Record.
    Jerome S. Handler and Michael L. Tuite Jr. Virginia Foundation for the
    Humanities and Digital Media Lab at the University of Virginia Library.
    http://hitchcock.itc.virginia.edu/Slavery/

British History 1700–1930: The Slave Trade. Spartacus Internet Encyclopedia.
    © 2005 Spartacus Educational.
    http://www.spartacus.schoolnet.co.uk/slavery.htm

Bibliography

Appiah, Kwame Anthony, and Henry Louis Gates Jr., eds. *Africana: The
    Encyclopedia of the African and African American Experience.* New York:
    Basic Civitas Books, 1999.

Bailey, Anne C. *African Voices of the Atlantic Slave Trade.* Boston: Beacon
    Press, 2005.

Camara, Abdoulaye, and Joseph Roger deBenoist. *Gorée: The Island and the Historical Museum.* Dakar, Senegal: IFAN-Cheikh Anta Diop and the Historical Museum, 1993.

Conneau, Theophilus. *A Slaver's Log Book, or Twenty Years' Residence in Africa.* First published 1854. Reprint, Englewood Cliffs, NJ: Avon/Prentice Hall, 1976.

Davidson, Basil. *The African Slave Trade.* Boston: Little, Brown, 1980.

Diene, Doudou, ed. *From Chains to Bonds: The Slave Trade Revisited.* New York: Berghahn, 2001.

Howard, Thomas, ed. *Black Voyage: Eyewitness Accounts of the Atlantic Slave Trade.* Boston: Little, Brown, 1971.

Jones, Howard. *Mutiny on the* Amistad: *The Saga of a Slave Revolt and Its Impact on American Abolition, Law, and Diplomacy.* New York: Oxford University Press, 1987.

Roberson, Erriel D. *The Maafa and Beyond.* Columbia, MD: Kujichagulia, 1995.

Sharp, S. Pearl. *The Healing Passage: Voices from the Water.* VHS. Los Angeles, CA: A Sharp Show, 2004. (www.asharpshow.com)

Van Sertima, Ivan. *They Came before Columbus.* New York: Random House, 1976.

Index